This book

belongs to

Harriet

Ferrari

PEOPLE OF THE WILLOW

PEOPLE OF THE WILLOW

The Padlimiut Tribe of the Caribou Eskimo

Portrayed in watercolours by

WINIFRED PETCHEY MARSH

Toronto OXFORD UNIVERSITY PRESS 1976

THIS BOOK IS DEDICATED
TO THE MEMORY OF MY HUSBAND
DONALD BEN MARSH
TO OUR CHILDREN DAVID, ROSEMARY, AND VALERIE
AND TO OUR BELOVED INUIT

ISBN 19-540271-5

234-987

Printed in Hong Kong by
EVERBEST PRINTING COMPANY LIMITED

Introduction

'The Padlimiut themselves assert that their name is not taken from any particular locality, but from the many willow bushes in their country, which in fact are more luxuriant than those of the other tribes. The word (padlei) means "willow"'. – KAJ BIRKETT-SMITH: The Caribou Eskimo

In the summer of 1933, as a young bride just arrived from England, I went to live at Eskimo Point on the western shore of Hudson Bay. My husband, the Reverend Donald Marsh, had already been living there for seven years. We had grown up together in England, north of London. Early in the 1920s, long before we were engaged to be married, Donald had been accepted by the Colonial and Continental Missionary Society, which was particularly active in Canada at the time. He had gone from England to study at Emmanuel College, Saskatoon, where he was trained for the ministry, and in 1926 he offered himself for Arctic service in the diocese of Keewatin, which in those

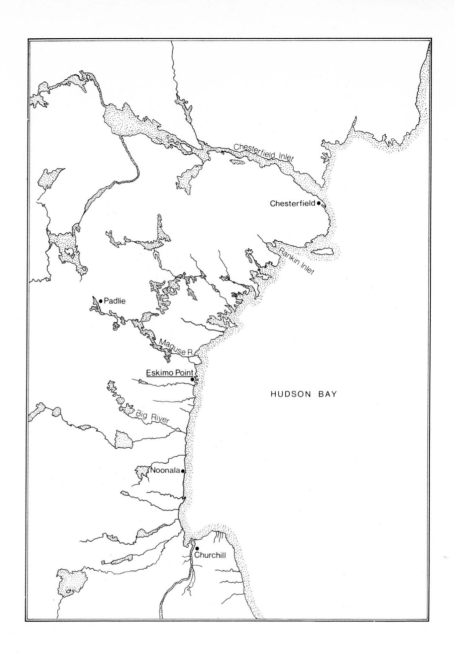

days stretched from Kenora to the North Pole. By the time I came to Eskimo Point seven years later–one of the first white women to live north of Churchill–my husband was already an experienced Arctic hand, though he was only a year older than myself. He spoke fluent Eskimo, acting not only as a preacher and teacher, but also as doctor, dentist, builder, furniture-maker, undertaker, and friend to the Eskimos, the white trappers, and others who lived in the North. By contrast I was a completely untried young woman who had just spent the last three years teaching art in North London, and the prospect of my new life was the opening of another world.

The first Anglican mission at Eskimo Point had been built by my husband seven years earlier. The material for it had come from the old jail in Churchill, which had been floated up the coast by whaleboat. A new house was built that we had designed together in England. The community of Eskimo Point in 1933 consisted of the Hudson's Bay Company post and the Anglican and Roman Catholic missions, along with a collection of Eskimo tents. About two Eskimo families lived there throughout the year, while as many as three hundred and fifty Padlimiut collected each summer, leaving in the early fall to hunt caribou and later trap white foxes.

I found that the mission was much more than a preaching outpost and that our house would be more than an ordinary home. It was a centre of continual labour and service. In those early years the missions–of whatever denomination–and occasionally the Hudson's Bay posts also, provided the only medical, dental, or educational services available. Ours was one of many such missions scattered through the Arctic. A yearly grant of two hundred dollars was paid by the Canadian government to our diocese for our services to the local inhabitants. The Department of Indian Affairs supplied us with

basic medicines and the rest we bought ourselves. My husband received a stipend of one thousand dollars a year from the Church of England in Canada, and when he married me this was increased by two hundred dollars a year as a wife's allowance. For the rest, in later years we were to supplement this income as best we could from his photography, which was sold to magazines and geographical societies, and by the sale of a few of my pictures. In all I suppose we managed on a good deal less than two thousand dollars a year. We had to live simply. Freight from the south in 1933 cost sixty dollars a ton, and since we needed at least six tons of coal a year for heating, we could not afford to bring in much food. Fresh potatoes and a hundred pounds of onions were almost our only fresh staples. Canned goods were luxuries, so I kept them for birthdays and special occasions. In the early years we brought in a year's supply of eggs packed in salt. For the most part we had dried vegetables. Sometimes we might receive a gift of fresh apples in the summer. When my son was small we began to import oranges for him. We traded flour, sugar, and tea for caribou and fishmeat.

My husband and I had both taken medical training at Livingstone College in London to prepare for our new life in Canada's North. We had paid for this ourselves. Our courses included dentistry at Bethnel Green Medical Clinic and midwifery, which I pursued for additional experience at the Mother's Hospital in London. We had done practical out-patient work at the Mildmay Mission. Though we felt ourselves to be unskilled, and though I was so inexperienced, I found that such skills as we had were constantly in demand once we were on our own at the mission. On one occasion I had to extract my husband's wisdom teeth, and dissolved in tears when the job was done. I also delivered babies. During the winter, school was held in our kitchen every day from two till four, followed by music and singing lessons. (It was held in the schoolroom in summer.) The Eskimos learned to read and write in their own language and we also taught English and simple mathematics. Sermons in church were very practical and were always inspired by a respect for the Eskimo way of life.

By the fall our fresh supplies would begin to go rotten and we would find that the cases of eggs held many that were cracked, broken, or bad. To prevent further wastage and to provide against the winter, I made many pounds of mincemeat, lemon-curd filling, and Christmas cakes—the latter to go into Christmas parcels for some of the men who were living alone, such as the white trappers in the district.

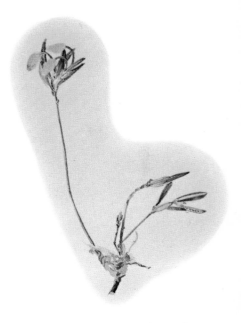

Call it what you will—shyness, over-sensitivity, or an unwillingness to pry into another people's way of life—I was hesitant to portray in pictures the life of the people to whom I had come, and who soon held for me such a great appeal. At first I sat in a corner unobtrusively and made notes or studied dress ornamentations while the Padlimiut visited. Later, from an open window, it was possible to study and record the sky, land, sea, or people. When the Eskimos saw and understood what I was doing, they became very interested and helped me as much as possible. For example, they built an igloo at our doorstep in which I could study the form and colour effects of anyone who would pose for me.

I was consumed with the desire to share my experiences with those less privileged than I who were unlikely ever to see the beauty and hardness of life as lived by the Padlimiut. I chose watercolour painting as a means of expression because of the need for speed and clarity of colour, and each painting became a prayer. I always had to work quickly, sometimes at

temperatures of forty degrees below zero. I sketched around the settlement of Eskimo Point, using mostly coloured pencils. After having firmly established my impression of the subject, I would at once transfer it to prepared paper, using watercolour. This was done within the comfort of home. Sometimes, as in 'A Northern Igloo', we made more heat by increasing the number of lighted wicks of the *koodlerk* (blubber lamp), making it comfortable for me to paint people, puppies, snow benches, and drying racks to my heart's content.

There was no blubber lamp and no heat in a Padlimiut igloo, so my paintings of igloo interiors were done at the very end of winter, when the spring thaw had set in–a bit uncomfortable when icy drips fell down my neck and odours were a little high. One year I was glad that I had persevered, because next morning not an igloo was left – they had all collapsed overnight.

Sometimes in mid-July, while painting along the coastline, my brush would suddenly become unmanageable and the painting would look as if a stone had broken a pane of glass across the sky. The painting had frozen.

As soon as the days became warm enough in the spring, the women began to dry out the deerskins that had been shot during the winter, before storing them away for use the next winter. Fox furs were suspended from poles and lines to whiten and dry in the sunshine and wind. When the men went off sealing and walrus hunting, a party of women would often go to gather 'wood'. This consisted of mosses intermingled with twigs and dried plants from the previous year's growth. On these occasions the younger children, who stayed at home in the charge of older sisters, always knew how to make the most of life, even if it was only collecting old tin cans and playing 'store' in the sand. Some scoured the land for berries; others collected cranberry leaves, which they scorched in a frying pan and gave to their parents for tobacco. Almost every boy shaped his own boat and then proudly sailed it on the lake behind our house – it was a pretty sight to see these miniature whaling boats racing under a stiff breeze. Or young lads, either with the permission of their parents or simply from boyish daring, would take their fathers' canoes and sail on the lakes. I remember once seeing two canoes, each holding two boys, having a race. The losers finally ran onto a little sandy edge with their boat half full of water. I can still see them standing waist deep in the lake in their deerskin clothing, making a vain effort to turn the canoe on its side to drain it.

All the words in the world could never have expressed for me the secret of the charm of that land. The Barren Lands were formed from an old seabed left from the Ice Age. They are as flat as the unbroken surface of a pond, with some outcroppings of rock here and there along the coastline, extending into Hudson Bay and forming shallows and uncharted reefs. Even in June there might still be no flowers, only exceptionally large willow blossoms. The tiny trunks of these willow shrubs, only a quarter of an inch thick, trailed across the land and in time became embedded in the mosses, so that the pussy willows had a wonderfully soft green background to set off their first shiny silver blossoms, which later turned yellow with pollen. Other willow shrubs, though smaller, appeared a beautiful pink. As I sat among them sketching, I was surrounded by a delicate fragrance.

Cushions of flowers, in solid massed colour, grew in the summer months on little patches of fine gravel. Blue gentians were scattered around the edges. Lovely flowers covered all the land and the old beach levels so that it

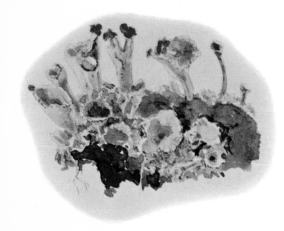

was impossible not to walk on wild rhododendrons, saxifrage, lesser willowherb, and other Alpine varieties. Walking in hidden depressions and on lower ground levels, the unwary might suddenly plunge into deep mosses of all kinds, with vivid colours and luxuriant growth. Often these areas led directly into grasses, sedges, water, and finally into a shallow sandy-bottomed lake. Around the edges of the water nested eider and other ducks, a variety of geese, ptarmigan and smaller birds, while the red-throated loon lay claim to small islands or promontories. The landscape was mirrored in the quiet water. Over all hung the soft, sweet-smelling air from the tundra, blending with the tang of the sea. The awesome silence and stillness were broken only by the gabbling of ducks or the shrill cry of tern or snipe.

The Hudson's Bay Company supply ship from Fort Churchill made her last trip to Eskimo Point at the end of August. Glorious weather continued until the end of October, when rapid climatic changes took place. Snow fell, usually during the night, and it was sufficient to make all the land white. Within a few days the water in the lakes was frozen to the depth of about a foot. The ice was clear as crystal and perfectly safe to walk upon. It was fun to peer through it and see small fish swimming around in the water beneath.

With the change in the weather everyone became busy. Those of us who required lots of water for the winter cut several tons of ice blocks from the lakes and stacked them near our houses. In answer to a smoke signal from inland the resident Padlimiut—who were mostly employed as fur cleaners—hitched up their dogs and went off on their sleds to hunt and kill deer for winter food. At home the children were training wee puppies to pull sleds. All day long they trailed up and down the lakes, with perhaps one or two pups hitched to a miniature sled. Flocks of birds passed overhead, densely packed. With the shirr of many wings they sped upon their way, leaving behind them a strange and solemn stillness – the land seemed suddenly desolate and void of life when they had gone.

In November, days of intense cold brought great changes to the land and sea. The wind stripped off much of the snow, leaving only long, tail-like drifts. The sea was frozen for about six miles out. All this happened very quickly. The water along the shore froze first, and then the next high tide came and washed some of the ice away, causing it to float loose near the land. The tide receded and again the water along the shore would freeze, till the next high tide carried on the work of washing away a certain amount of ice. Gradually, as the month proceeded, the shore extended far out and the floating ice became so compact that the bay was filled. Over the open water there was always a haze, which from a distance made the sky look dark and forbidding.

The Padlimiut worked very hard during the winter. The men were up and away at daybreak to make the round of their traps, always hoping they would be rewarded with a good catch of white fox. The traps had to be kept in good order, and each sled in perfect condition. The sled runners were glazed with frozen mud by hand – not an easy job in a country where the temperature would be fifty degrees below zero or even lower still.

The sleds made a thrilling sight at Christmas time when a great number of them glided into the settlement bringing Eskimo men from the north, south and west, all eager to assemble together to keep their Christmas festival and to trade their pelts. The women and children stayed behind in their inland camps. (At the best of times family travel was always a major undertak-

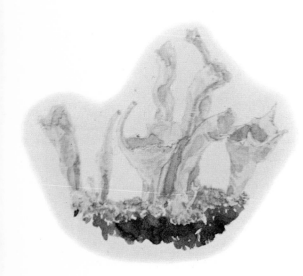

ing, and in winter it was impossible.) Nature gave of her best to reproduce again the setting for the holy night. The land was silent and still and there was one huge glorious star close to the moon that shone with particular beauty between the twilight and the dark, while the sky across the western horizon was that mysterious blue-green that fades into the pale yellow and gold of sunset. The Northern Lights seemed to hang in a complete circle overhead. At daybreak the snow lay deep and stretched away to the horizon; to the north it looked cold and forbidding. A large three-quarter moon rode high in the heavens. In the east a shallow arch of rosy light proclaimed the birth of Christmas Day. The temperature would be about forty degrees below zero. The radio brought a real whiff of the Christmas spirit right into our home, and I cannot tell what a joy it was for us to have a radio set at Christmas time. We turned night into day when we sat up to listen to the programs of messages broadcast to the men in the North, both from Canada and the United States, and we enjoyed many of the English programs and the Christmas broadcasts around the world. We had lovely services that were followed later on Christmas morning by a great feast for the Eskimos of steaming hot stew, rice pudding, and gallons of tea.

At the threshold of the New Year we looked ahead to plan our work at Eskimo Point. My husband went by dogteam to visit all his people in their igloos, making three trips to do this, and sometimes staying away for six weeks at a time. Thus he remained close to all his parishioners before the Padlimiut returned again with their families to camp for the spring and summer. Meanwhile we were happy, doing whatever we could to make the lives of those around us brighter and less lonely.

Frequently I would find small cards attached to my painting board with typed sentences such as 'I know I am an artist'. This was Don's way of encouraging me and keeping me at it. By the spring it would be light at seven thirty in the morning and often, when he was away, I painted until six at night without neglecting the work of the mission. We enjoyed very clear bright light, so that I had to wear the Eskimo bone snow-goggles when sketching outside. These had slits to see through and no lenses; unlike the sunglasses of those days, they did not distort the colours. The snow glittered with thousands of tiny crystal facets – the loveliest diamonds one could wish to see. Working at my painting, in one week I completed a set of twenty drawings in black and white for a medical dictionary in Eskimo that Don had prepared. One day a small boy came in while I was drawing an anatomical skeleton. He pondered it for a while and then asked me, 'What did you do with all his meat, Mrs. Marsh?'

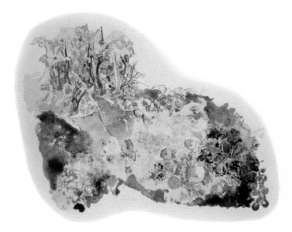

I had never seen such blizzards as I came to know now. It would get darker and darker in the house while the snow swirled thick in the air outside and piled higher against the walls and windows. Sometimes our house would be completely buried. Then it was as black as the nethermost pit, with the storm still raging outside. In the morning Don would open the back door onto a solid wall of snow. He would dig his way up and out to the open air and then back eight feet to the kitchen window. One day I saw an Eskimo mother and baby in beaded coat standing beyond this cave entrance of snow, against a clear blue sky. The woman and child were a jewel of colour and interest. I thought to myself, 'If only I can do it! What a subject!' I called this painting *Arctic Cameo.*

Often I have been asked how I got my models and kept them with me while I sketched them. It was quite simple once I had found the way. I would make cocoa so boiling hot that it took my visitors a long time to drink, and while they chatted and let the cocoa cool, I painted them.

After my son was born, nothing thrilled him so much as to see me painting. My art was something that could so easily have been crowded out of my life, and without my husband's co-operation I think it would have been.

Perhaps of all the paintings I did, the drum dance caused the greatest sensation. I decided to do it after we had been invited to attend a drum dance. We reconstructed a section of the dance tent in our school room and set up lighting effects there. Throughout the winter, members of our congregation and visitors to our settlement willingly posed so that they might be in the picture. I had over forty models for portraits, but my husband should really take the credit for this particular painting, for he kept me at it, even until eleven o'clock one night. It was possible to sketch only when the Eskimos were visiting the post, which was about three times during the winter. The whole painting had to be done in artificial light, similar to the lighting effect inside a double caribou skin tent. Yet in spite of that, I believe it remains a true picture of Eskimo life.

We saw the Arctic change. My husband died in 1973 after forty-seven years of service, first as a missionary, and then as Anglican Bishop of the Arctic. The way of life recorded in my paintings has gone now from the country of the Padlimiut, and perhaps will soon have vanished everywhere. Yet the land and the people remain, many of them living in dedicated service to God and their fellow men. Sure in the knowledge of this, my present life is filled with thankfulness and praise.

Scenes of Padlimiut Life

Padlimiut summer camp

Gathering moss in the summer

Cleaning seal skins in the summer

Largest-known Padlimiut soapstone cooking-pot

Padlimiut grave of a drowned man

23

Summer school at Eskimo Point

Drum Dance at Eskimo Point

Inside a Padlimiut summer tent

Snowy day in early summer   27

Starting the fall migration

Cache for autumn storage

Ice craters (collection Dr & Mrs Bonar)

Sea ice forming in the fall on Hudson Bay

Padlimiut camp life in the fall

Mudding a sled outside an ice igloo

Padlimiut snow igloo with snow porch

Padlimiut washday: drying skins   35

Aivilingmiut (northern) dome-shaped igloos

Padlimiut winter encampment

Arctic cameo

Patoongnuya coming into an igloo

Ootooyuk chopping deermeat in her home

Arrival of a visitor

Oolaryoo preparing some food

Eeyak's widow with one of seven children

Ortukaryooak the Inlander

Heeootoroot with hairsticks

Winter fishing for char and lake trout

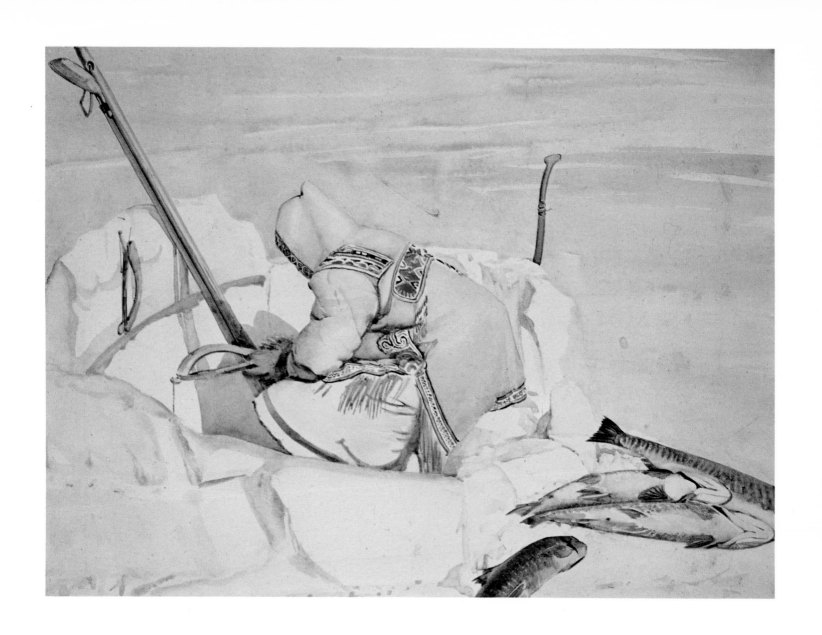

Spring fish-jigging at an icehole

Unloading willow twigs by the snow chimney of an underground composite igloo

Willow-twig fire in the kitchen of the same composite igloo

Repairing a caribou-skin tent tarpaulin in early spring

Willows in a pool near two Padlimiut graves   51

Beaded Appliqué Clothes and Ornaments of the Padlimiut and Aivilingmiut Peoples

The following paintings were made at Eskimo Point in 1933 and 1934. For more information on the lifestyle of the Padlimiut, the reader is referred to Kaj Birkett Smith: The Caribou Eskimo, *to the Manitoba Museum of Man and Nature, and to the National Museum of Man.*

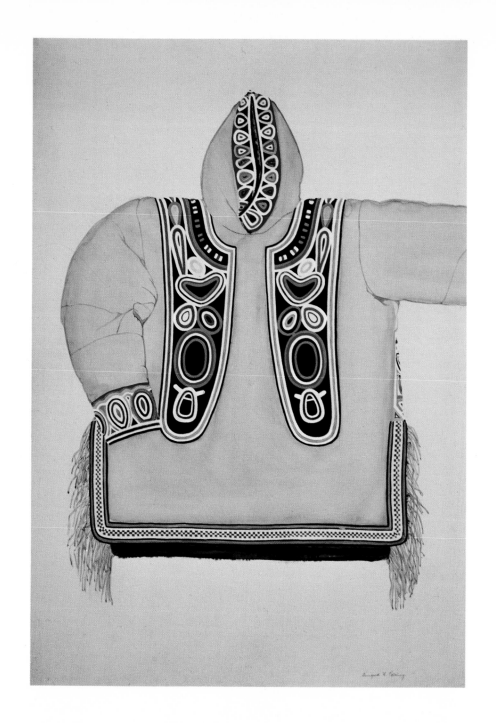

*Padlimiut man's **attigi** or inner coat (front view). Note the absence of a bottom fringe—this was taboo on the coast*

Padlimiut man's **attigi** *or inner coat (rear view)*

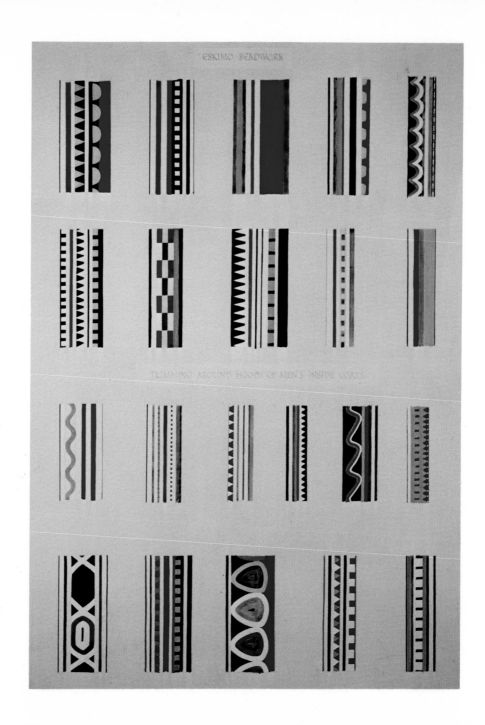

Padlimiut beadwork borders for hoods and cuffs

Padlimiut hairsticks, headband, watchpocket, girl's puberty symbol, boy's
hood ornament, earrings, sewing pouch, and cuffbands

Padlimiut woman's **attigi** *or inner coat (front view)*

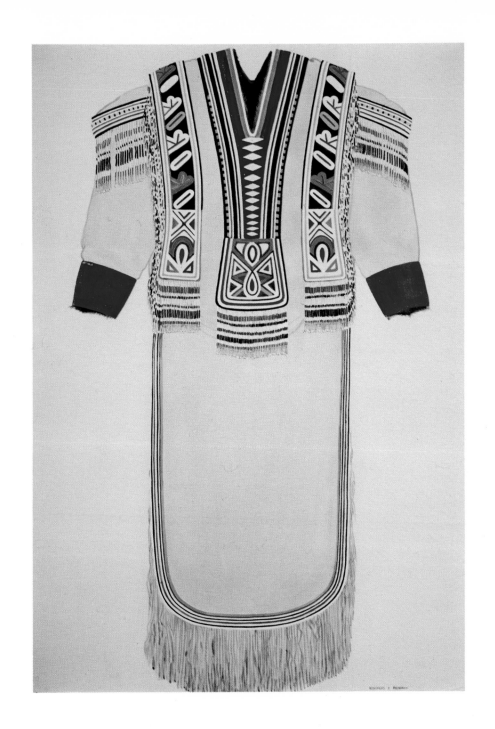

Padlimiut woman's **attigi** *or inner coat (rear view)*

Above

Beaded Applique Panel from the back
of a man's attigie (inside coat.)

Ornaments from the hood of the
attigie.   Inland Padlimiut.

Padlimiut attigi *back panel for a man (inlander) with* attigi *hood ornaments*

Padlimiut **attigi** *back panels for boys and men. The symbols in the third (boy's) row represent mosquitoes and the wearer's name*

Aivilingmiut woman's attigi *or inner coat (front view)*

Aivilingmiut woman's attigi *or inner coat (rear view)*

To commemorate the Silver Jubilee of

Her Majesty Queen Elizabeth II

the National Chapter of Canada, IODE, has purchased

the Marsh Collection of Watercolours

for presentation to the new

Territorial Central Museum, Yellowknife, NWT

1977